Piano • Vocal • Guitar

Contemporary Christian Christmas

ISBN 0-634-01910-4

7777 W. BLUEMOUND RD. P.O. BOX 13819 MILWAUKEE, WI 53213

For all works contained herein:
Unauthorized copying, arranging, adapting, recording or public performance is an infringement of copyright.
Infringers are liable under the law.

Visit Hal Leonard Online at
www.halleonard.com

Contemporary Christian
Christmas

ALL IS WELL

Words and Music by MICHAEL W. SMITH
and WAYNE KIRKPATRICK

Meditative ♩ = 76

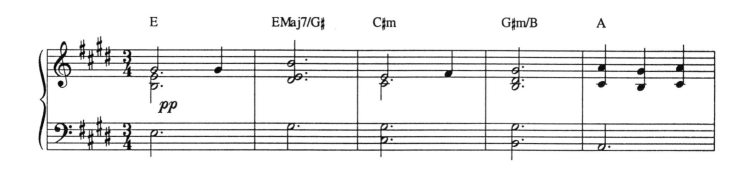

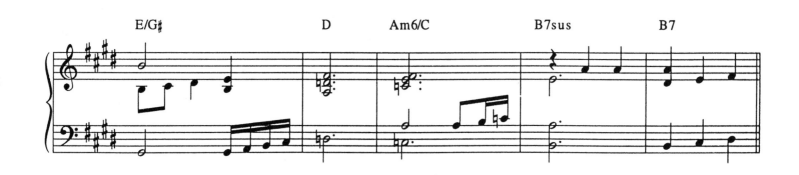

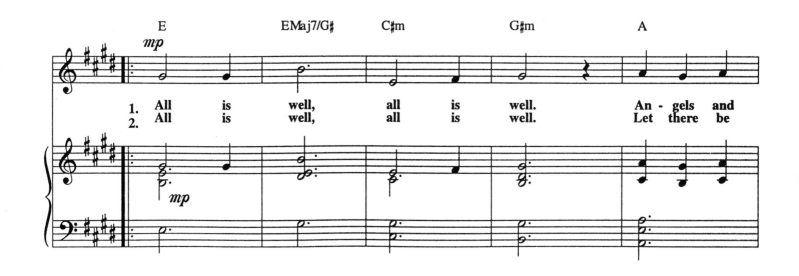

1. All is well, all is well. An-gels and
2. All is well, all is well. Let there be

Copyright © 1989 by Milene Music, Inc. and Careers-BMG Music Publishing, Inc.
All Rights Reserved   Used by Permission

BETHLEHEM MORNING

Words and Music by
MORRIS CHAPMAN

© 1982 Word Music, Inc. and Garpax Music Press (admin. by Word Music, Inc.)
All Rights Reserved   Used by Permission

BE IT UNTO ME

Words and Music by RANDY PHILLIPS
and CINDY MORGAN

With energy ♩ = 95

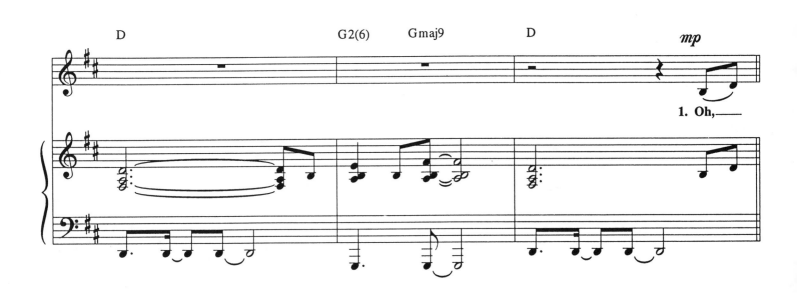

© 1996 ARIOSE MUSIC, WORLD OF PENTECOST and WORD MUSIC, INC.
ARIOSE MUSIC and WORLD OF PENTECOST Admin. by EMI CHRISTIAN MUSIC PUBLISHING
All Rights Reserved   Used by Permission

BREATH OF HEAVEN
(Mary's Song)

Words and Music by AMY GRANT
and CHRIS EATON

© 1992, 1997 SGO MUSIC PUBLISHING, LTD. (BMI) o/b/o CLOUSEAU MUSIC/
Administered by BUG MUSIC and AGE TO AGE MUSIC, INC. (ASCAP)/Administered by THE LOVING COMPANY
All Rights Reserved   Used by Permission

CELEBRATE THE CHILD

Words and Music by
MICHAEL CARD

In four with a beat

© 1986 BIRDWING MUSIC and MOLE END MUSIC
Admin. by EMI CHRISTIAN MUSIC PUBLISHING
All Rights Reserved   Used by Permission

EMMANUEL

Words and Music by
MICHAEL W. SMITH

© 1983 MEADOWGREEN MUSIC COMPANY
Admin. by EMI CHRISTIAN MUSIC PUBLISHING
All Rights Reserved   Used by Permission

CHILD OF BETHLEHEM

Words by WAYNE WATSON and CLAIRE CLONINGER
Music by WAYNE WATSON

© 1994 Word Music, Inc., Juniper Landing Music (admin. by Word Music, Inc.) and Material Music (admin. by Word Music, Inc.)
All Rights Reserved Used by Permission

Child of Beth - le - hem is the King of_____ kings!

Still, wise men wor - ship at His_____ feet,_____ and lost souls a - wak - en

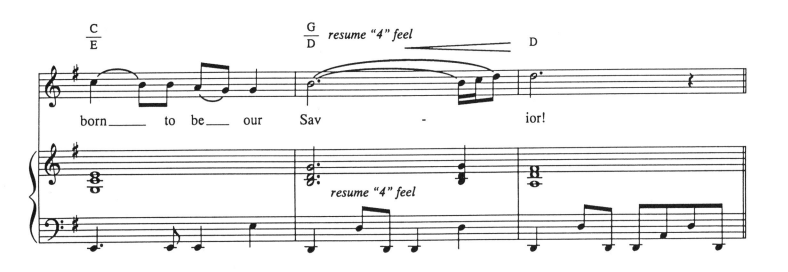

GOING HOME FOR CHRISTMAS

Words and Music by STEVEN CURTIS CHAPMAN
and JAMES ISAAC ELLIOT

Rhythmically and flowing

Her
house was where ___ the fam - 'ly gath - ered ev 'ry Christ - mas eve. ___
year the leaves ___ be - gan ___ to fall and her health be - gan ___ to fail. ___
leaves out - side ___ have fall - en to be cov - ered by ___ the snow. ___

The feast was on ___ the ta -
We moved her to ___ a place
The fam - 'ly comes ___ with food ___

© 1995 SPARROW SONG, PEACH HILL SONGS and CABINETMAKER MUSIC (ASCAP)/Admin. by ICG
SPARROW SONG and PEACH HILL SONGS Admin. by EMI CHRISTIAN MUSIC PUBLISHING
All Rights Reserved   Used by Permission

And she is home, _____ she's home for Christ - mas. _____

GOOD NEWS

Words and Music by
ROB MATHES

Original key: A♭ major. This edition has been transposed down one half-step to be more playable.

© 1995 RIVER OAKS MUSIC and MAYBE I CAN MUSIC
Admin. by EMI CHRISTIAN MUSIC PUBLISHING
All Rights Reserved   Used by Permission

IMMANUEL

Words and Music by
MICHAEL CARD

With hope

1. A sign shall be giv-en, a vir-gin will__ con-
(2.) What shall be your an-swer? Oh, will you hear__ the

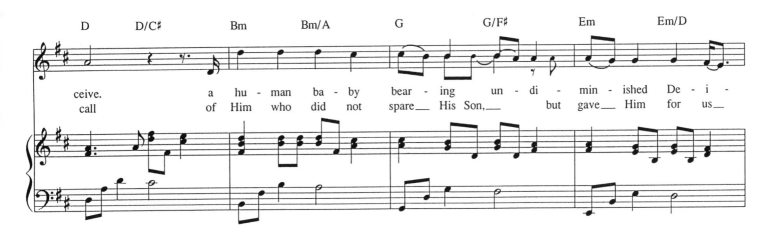

ceive. a hu-man ba-by bear-ing un-di-min-ished De-i-
call of Him who did not spare__ His Son,__ but gave__ Him for us__

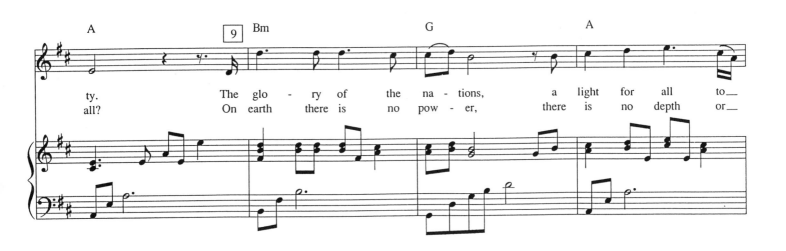

ty. The glo-ry of the na-tions, a light for all to__
all? On earth there is no pow-er, there is no depth or__

© 1986 BIRDWING MUSIC and MOLE END MUSIC
Admin. by EMI CHRISTIAN MUSIC PUBLISHING
All Rights Reserved   Used by Permission

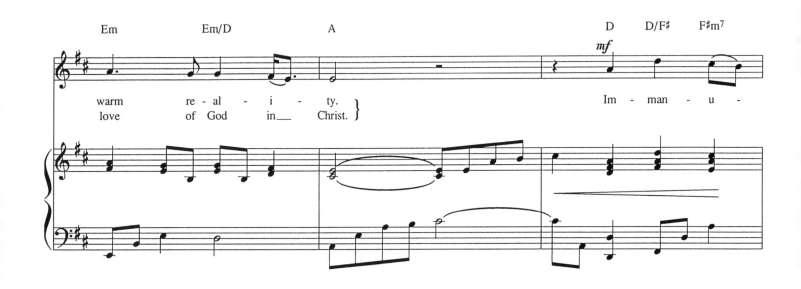

JESUS IS BORN

Words and Music by STEVE GREEN,
PHIL NAISH and COLLEEN GREEN

© 1987 BIRDWING MUSIC, PAMELA KAY MUSIC, BECKENGUS MUSIC and BMG SONGS, INC.
BIRDWING MUSIC, PAMELA KAY MUSIC and BECKENGUS MUSIC Admin. by EMI CHRISTIAN MUSIC PUBLISHING
All Rights Reserved   Used by Permission

JOY (TO THE WORLD)

Words and Music by DAN MUCKALA,
GRANT CUNNINGHAM and BROWN BANNISTER

© 2000 SPARROW SONG, IMAGINE THIS MUSIC, DESIGNER MUSIC, INC. and RBI MUSIC
SPARROW SONG and IMAGINE THIS MUSIC Admin. by EMI CHRISTIAN MUSIC PUBLISHING
DESIGNER MUSIC, INC. Admin. by BRENTWOOD-BENSON MUSIC PUBLISHING, INC.
All Rights Reserved   Used by Permission

ONE SMALL CHILD

Words and Music by
DAVID MEECE

One small child in a land of a thou - sand,
One small child in a land of a thou - sand,

one small dream of a Sav - ior to - night.
one small dream in a peo - ple of might.

One small hand reach-ing out to the star - light, one small cit - y of
One small hand reach-ing out to the star - light, one small Sav - ior of

© 1971 Word Music, Inc.
All Rights Reserved Used by Permission

PRECIOUS PROMISE

Words and Music by
STEVEN CURTIS CHAPMAN

Oh, what a pre - cious prom - ise, oh, what a gift __ of love; __
an an - gel tells __ a vir - gin that __

© 1995 SPARROW SONG and PEACH HILL SONGS
Admin. by EMI CHRISTIAN MUSIC PUBLISHING
All Rights Reserved   Used by Permission

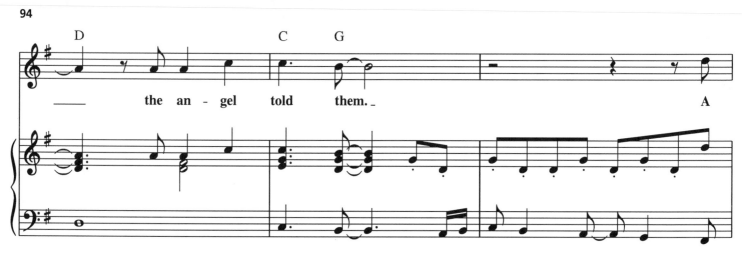

the an - gel told them. _____ A

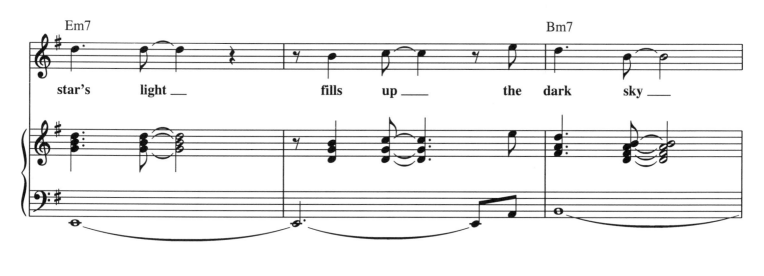

star's light ____ fills up ____ the dark sky ____

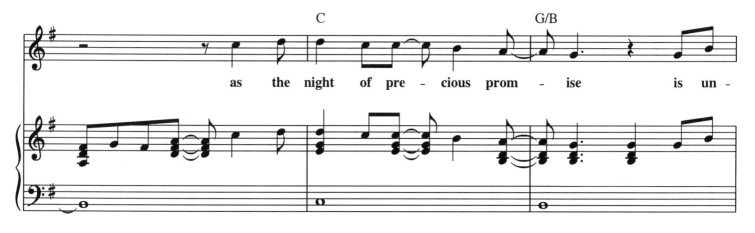

as the night of pre - cious prom - ise is un -

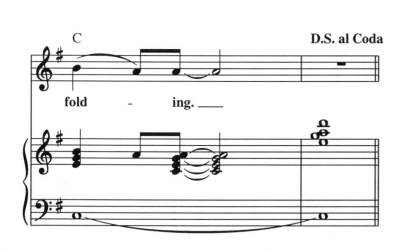

fold - ing. ____

D.S. al Coda

CODA

man - ger in Beth - le - hem. ____

ROSE OF BETHLEHEM

Words and Music by
LOWELL ALEXANDER

© 1992 BIRDWING MUSIC
Admin. by EMI CHRISTIAN MUSIC PUBLISHING
All Rights Reserved   Used by Permission

THIS BABY

Words and Music by
STEVEN CURTIS CHAPMAN

What child is this, __ who, laid to rest, __ on Ma - ry's lap __ is sleep - ing? Whom an - gels greet __ with an - thems sweet, __ while shep - herds watch __ are keep - ing?

© 1995 SPARROW SONG and PEACH HILL SONGS
Admin. by EMI CHRISTIAN MUSIC PUBLISHING
All Rights Reserved   Used by Permission

THIS GIFT

Words and Music by STEVE AMERSON
and DAVID T. CLYDESDALE

© 1994 Word Music, Inc. and Dayspring Music, Inc.
All Rights Reserved   Used by Permission

THIS LITTLE CHILD

Words and Music by
SCOTT WESLEY BROWN

Copyright © 1981 by Careers-BMG Music Publishing, Inc. and Sparrow Song
All Rights for Sparrow Song Admin. by EMI Christian Music Publishing
International Copyright Secured   All Rights Reserved

UNTO US
(Isaiah 9)

Words and Music by LARRY BRYANT
and LESA BRYANT

© 1990 STONEBROOK MUSIC COMPANY
Admin. by EMI CHRISTIAN MUSIC PUBLISHING
All Rights Reserved   Used by Permission

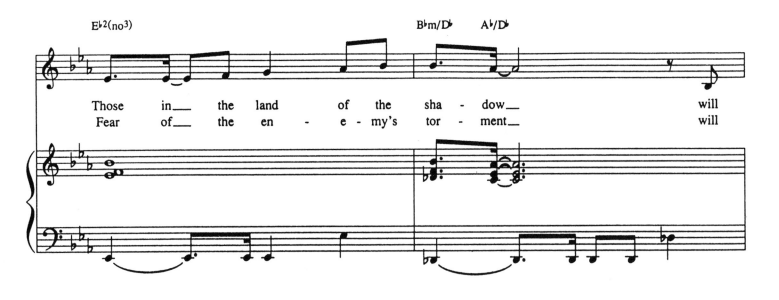

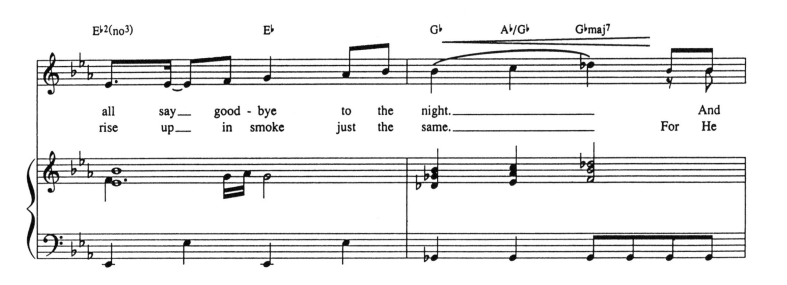

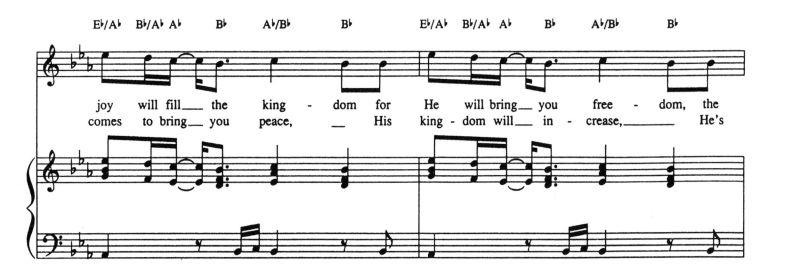

A STRANGE WAY TO SAVE THE WORLD

Words and Music by DAVE CLARK,
MARK HARRIS and DON KOCH

1. I'm sure he must have been   sur - prised   at where this road   had tak - en him.
(2.) could   have been   if Je - sus had come   as He de - served.

© 1993 John T. Benson Publishing Co., Paragon Music Corp., Point Clear Music,
New Spring Publishing, Inc. (ASCAP) (all admin. by Brentwood-Benson Music Publishing, Inc.)
and A-Knack-For-This Music (ASCAP) (admin. by ICG)
All Rights Reserved   Used by Permission

136